MARK TWAIN'S
Huckleberry Wisdom

The Wit and Wisdom of Mark Twain

COLLEEN SATTLER

CONTENTS

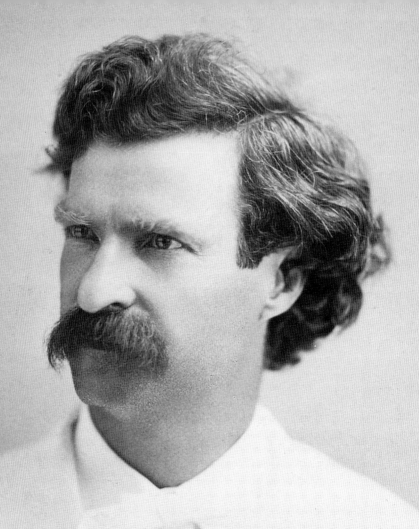

S.L. Clemens
Mark Twain

Mark Twain

Originally christened Samuel Clemens, Mark Twain was a humorist, entrepreneur, adventurer, publisher, public speaker and animal lover. He is celebrated as 'the father of American literature' and revered for his colloquial adventure stories. His friendly, funny and irreverent style brought him great success as a writer and a paid speaker. Performing many humorous talks, he paved the way for modern stand-up comedians.

During his life, Mark Twain knew great happiness and profound sorrow, immense riches and painful bankruptcy. Combined with these life experiences, radical views and wily intellect, his words of wisdom still speak to us today.

This book contains a selection of outrageous quotes about life taken from Twain's writings, speeches and conversations. So sit back and enjoy the radical, homespun wisdom of Mark Twain. Be astonished, amused and entertained.

ANIMALS VERSUS HUMANS

If you pick up a starving dog
and make him prosperous,
he will not bite you. This is the
principal difference between
a dog and a man.

– Pudd'nhead Wilson

Heaven goes by favor.
If it went by merit,
you would stay out and
your dog would go in.

– In a note

Very often, in matters concerning religion and politics a man's reasoning powers are not above the monkey's.

– Mark Twain's Autobiography

13

It is just like man's vanity and impertinence to call an animal dumb because it is dumb to his dull perceptions.

– What is Man?

Man is the only animal
that blushes. Or needs to.

— Pudd'nhead Wilson

If man could be crossed with the cat it would improve man, but it would deteriorate the cat.

— *Mark Twain's Notebook*

A cat is more intelligent than people believe, and can be taught any crime.

– *Mark Twain's Notebook*

One of the most striking differences between a cat and a lie is that a cat has only nine lives.

– *Pudd'nhead Wilson*

TRUTH
AND
LIES

If you tell the truth you don't have to remember anything.

— *Mark Twain's Notebook*

An awkward, feeble, leaky lie is a thing which you ought ... to avoid ... Why, you might as well tell the truth at once and be done with it.

– During a speech

Always acknowledge a fault frankly. This will throw those in authority off their guard and give you opportunity to commit more.

— In a note

Honesty is the best policy –
when there is money in it.

– During a speech

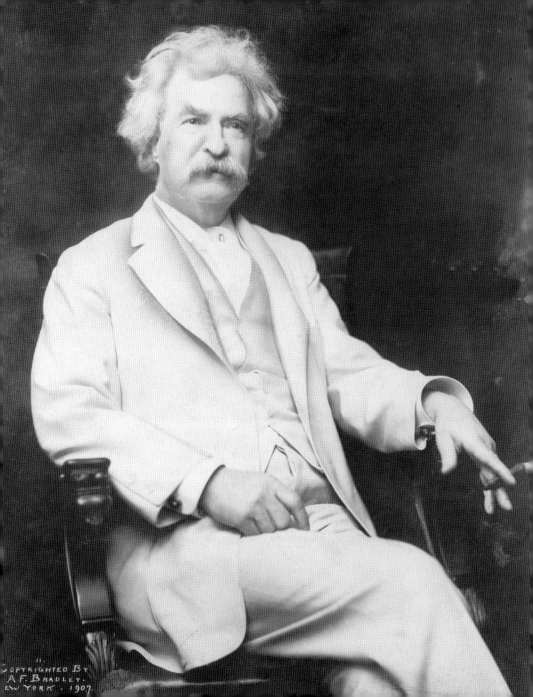

MONEY

What is the chief end of man?
– To get rich. In what way?
– Dishonestly if we can;
honestly if we must.

– *The Revised Catechism, New-York Tribune*

What's the use you learning to
do right when it's troublesome
to do right and ain't no trouble
to do wrong ...

— *Adventures of Huckleberry Finn*

Principles have no real force
except when one is well fed ...

– Extracts from Adams's Diary

Let us not be too particular.
It is better to have old
second-hand diamonds
than none at all.

– *Pudd'nhead Wilson*

Any so-called material thing
that you want is merely a
symbol: you want it not
for itself, but because it will
content your spirit for the
moment.

– What is Man?

I'm opposed to millionaires,
but it would be dangerous
to offer me the position.

– The American Claimant

SUCCESS

All you need in this life is ignorance and confidence; then success is sure.

– In a letter

The less a man knows
the bigger the noise he
makes and the higher the
salary he commands.

– How I Edited an Agricultural Paper

Human nature is the same
everywhere: it defies success,
it has nothing but scorn
for defeat.

— Personal Recollections of Joan of Arc

Let us be thankful for the
fools. But for them the rest
of us could not succeed.

– *Pudd'nhead Wilson*

Keep away from people who
try to belittle your ambitions.
Small people always do
that, but the really great
make you feel that you, too,
can become great.

— In conversation

A man has no business to be depressed by a disappointment, anyway; he ought to make up his mind to get even.

– *A Connecticut Yankee in King Arthur's Court*

Men's misfortunes are
forgotten in the excitement
of new enterprises.

– The Adventures of Tom Sawyer

WORK

Work consists of whatever
a body is obliged to do ...
Play consists of whatever
a body is not obliged to do.

— The Adventures of Tom Sawyer

Diligence is a good thing,
but taking things easy is
much more – restful.

– During a speech

My idea is that the employer
should be the busy man,
and the employee the idle one.
The employer should be the
worried man, and the employee
the happy one.

– *During a speech*

Never put off till tomorrow
what may be done [the] day
after tomorrow just as well.

– On a card

Do something every day
that you don't want to do.
This is the golden rule for
acquiring the habit of doing
your duty without pain.

— Pudd'nhead Wilson

POWER
OF
WORDS

There is nothing in the world
like a persuasive speech to
fuddle the mental apparatus
and upset the convictions
and debauch the emotions
of an audience ...

— *The Man that Corrupted Hadleyburg*

Many a small thing has been
made large by the right kind
of advertising.

– A Connecticut Yankee in King Arthur's Court

PACIFIC
WRECKING CO.

MARY'S
HOME
MADE
LUNCHES
25¢

HOME
MADE

LUNCHES
25¢

When angry, count four;
when very angry, swear.

— Pudd'nhead Wilson

The difference between the almost right word and the right word is really a large matter — 'tis the difference between the lightning-bug and the lightning.

— In a letter

Whenever we come upon one of those intensely right words in a book or a newspaper the resulting effect is physical as well as spiritual … it tingles exquisitely around through the walls of the mouth and tastes as tart and crisp and good as the autumn-butter that creams the sumac-berry.

– William Dean Howells

I notice that you use plain, simple language, short words and brief sentences. That is the way to write English … Stick to it; don't let fluff and flowers and verbosity creep in. When you catch an adjective, kill it.

— In a letter

PLEASURE

To promise not to do a thing is the surest way in the world to make a body want to go and do that very thing.

— The Adventures of Tom Sawyer

There is a charm about
the forbidden that makes it
unspeakably desirable.

— *Mark Twain's Notebook*

Good friends, good books
and a sleepy conscience:
this is the ideal life.

— Mark Twain's Notebook

Habit is habit, and not to
be flung out of the window
by any man, but coaxed
downstairs a step at a time.

— Pudd'nhead Wilson

I have never taken any exercise,
except sleeping and resting,
and I never intend to take any.
Exercise is loathsome.

– During a speech

Never refuse to do a kindness
unless the act would work
great injury to yourself, and
never refuse to take a drink —
under any circumstances.

— Mark Twain's Notebook

There are people who strictly deprive themselves of each and every eatable, drinkable, and smokable which has in any way acquired a shady reputation. They pay this price for health. And health is all they get for it. … It is like paying out your whole fortune for a cow that has gone dry.

— *Mark Twain's Autobiography*

The only way to keep your health is to eat what you don't want, drink what you don't like, and do what you'd druther not.

– Following the Equator

SEX

Many men are goats and can't
help committing adultery when
they get a chance; whereas
there are numbers of men
who … let an opportunity
go by if the woman lacks in
attractiveness.

– Letters from the Earth

The human being, like the immortals, naturally places sexual intercourse far and away above all other joys … The very thought of it excites him; opportunity sets him wild; in this state he will risk life, reputation, everything … to make good that opportunity and ride it to the overwhelming climax.

– Letters from the Earth

As an amusement
it [masturbation] is too
fleeting; as an occupation
it is too wearing;
as a public exhibition
there is no money in it.

– During a speech

If you must gamble away
your life sexually, don't play
a lone hand too much.

– During a speech

Familiarity breeds contempt –
and children.

– Mark Twain's Notebook

LOVE

When you fish for love,
bait with your heart,
not your brain.

— *Mark Twain's Notebook*

You can't reason with your heart; it has its own laws ... which the intellect scorns.

– *A Connecticut Yankee in King Arthur's Court*

Love is a madness;
if thwarted it develops fast.

— *The Memorable Assassination*

Men and women – even
man and wife are foreigners.
Each has reserves that the
other cannot enter into,
nor understand.

— *Mark Twain's Notebook*

There isn't time – so brief is life – for bickerings, apologies, heartburnings, callings to account. There is only time for loving ...

– In a letter

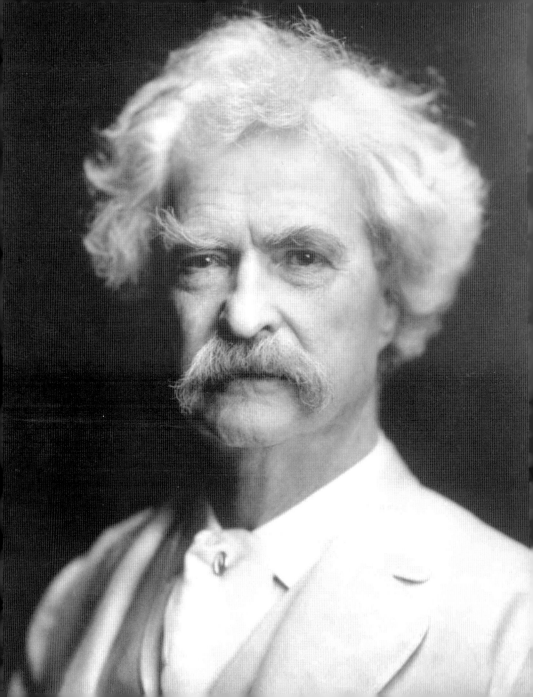

AGE
AND
LOOKS

As soon as a man recognizes that he has drifted into age, he gets reminiscent. He wants to talk and talk; and not about the present or the future, but about his old times. For there is where the pathos of his life lies — and the charm of it.

— Who is Mark Twain?

When a man is a pessimist
before 48 he knows too much;
if he is an optimist after it,
he knows too little.

– In a letter

Wrinkles should merely
indicate where smiles
have been.

– Pudd'nhead Wilson

Some civilized women
would lose half their charm
without dress, and some
would lose all of it.

– During a speech

Clothes make the man.
Naked people have little or
no influence in society.

– More Maxims of Mark by Merle Johnson

RELATIONSHIP WITH SELF

An occasional compliment is necessary to keep up one's self-respect … When you can't get a compliment any other way pay yourself one.

— *Mark Twain's Notebook*

I love compliments …
I can live on a good
compliment [for] two weeks
with nothing else to eat.

– *In a letter*

The best way to cheer
yourself is to try to
cheer somebody else up.

— *Mark Twain's Notebook*

Drag your thoughts away
from your troubles by the
ears, by the heels, or any other
way, so you manage it; it's the
healthiest thing a body can do;
dwelling on troubles is deadly,
just deadly ... You must keep
your mind amused ...

— *The American Claimant*

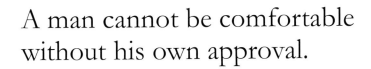

A man cannot be comfortable
without his own approval.

— *What is Man?*

When people do not
respect us we are sharply
offended; yet deep down
in his private heart no man
much respects himself.

– Pudd'nhead Wilson

We do not deal much in fact when we are contemplating ourselves.

– Does the Race of Man Love a Lord?

Whenever you find yourself
on the side of the majority,
it is time to reform –
(or pause and reflect).

– Mark Twain's Notebook

RELATIONSHIP WITH OTHERS

Always do right.
This will gratify some people
and astonish the rest.

– In a note

To be good is noble;
but to show others
how to be good is
nobler and no trouble.

– Following the Equator

Few things are harder
to put up with than
the annoyance of a
good example.

— Pudd'nhead Wilson

Nothing so needs reforming
as other people's habits.

— *Pudd'nhead Wilson*

Good breeding consists in
concealing how much we think
of ourselves and how little
we think of the other person.

– *Mark Twain's Notebook*

One should not pay a person
a compliment and straightway
follow it with a criticism.
It is better to kiss him now
and kick him next week.

– In an inscription

Do not offer a compliment and
ask a favor at the same time.
A compliment that is charged
for is not valuable.

– Mark Twain's Notebook

The holy passion of friendship
is of so sweet and steady and
loyal and enduring a nature
that it will last through a
whole lifetime, if not asked
to lend money.

— Pudd'nhead Wilson

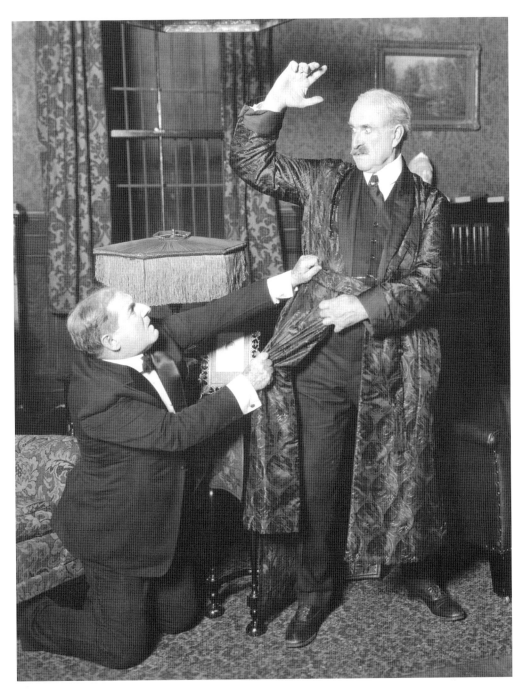

The proper office of a
friend is to side with you
when you are in the wrong.
Nearly anybody will side with
you when you are in the right.

— Mark Twain's Notebook

It takes your enemy and your
friend, working together,
to hurt you to the heart;
the one to slander you and the
other to get the news to you.

– *Following the Equator*

Each man is afraid of his
neighbor's disapproval —
a thing which, to the general
run of the race, is more
dreaded than wounds
and death.

— *The United States of Lyncherdom*

To get the full value of a joy
you must have somebody
to divide it with.

— Pudd'nhead Wilson

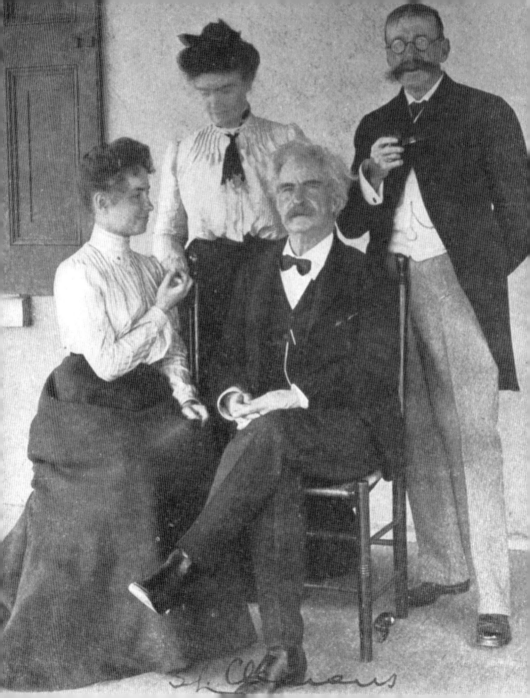

HUMAN
NATURE

To be envied is the secret
longing of pretty much
all human beings … to be
envied makes them happy.

– *No. 44, The Mysterious Stranger*

There are people who
can do all fine and heroic
things but one! Keep from
telling their happinesses
to the unhappy.

— *Pudd'nhead Wilson*

There are no people who
are quite so vulgar as the
over-refined ones.

– *Following the Equator*

Everyone is a moon,
and has a dark side which
he never shows to anybody.

— *Pudd'nhead Wilson*

The best of us would rather
be popular than right.

— No. 44, The Mysterious Stranger

We are discreet sheep; we wait
to see how the drove is going,
and then go with the drove.
We have two opinions: one
private, which we are afraid
to express; and another one
… which we force ourselves
to wear …

— *Mark Twain's Autobiography*

A round man cannot be
expected to fit a square hole
right away. He must have time
to modify his shape.

— Following the Equator

People are made different.
And it is the best way.

— *Tom Sawyer, Detective*

When we remember
that we are all mad, the
mysteries disappear and
life stands explained.

— *Mark Twain's Notebook*

Neither you, nor I, nor any man ever originates a thought in his own head. The utterer of a thought always utters a second-hand one.

— What is Man?

Life does not consist mainly –
or even largely – of facts and
happenings. It consists mainly
of the storm of thoughts that
is forever blowing through
one's head.

– Mark Twain's Autobiography

Travel is fatal to prejudice,
bigotry and narrow-
mindedness … Broad,
wholesome, charitable views
of men and things can not
be acquired by vegetating in
one little corner of the earth
all one's lifetime.

— *Innocents Abroad*

There ain't no surer way to
find out whether you like
people or hate them than
to travel with them.

— Tom Sawyer Abroad

WISDOM

A man should not be without morals; it is better to have bad morals than none at all.

– Mark Twain's Notebook

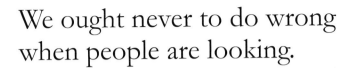

We ought never to do wrong
when people are looking.

– A Double-Barrelled Detective Story

Be good and you will
be lonesome.

– Following the Equator

Obscurity and a competence
– that is the life that is best
worth living.

– Mark Twain's Notebook

There was never yet an
uninteresting life. Such
a thing is an impossibility.
Inside of the dullest exterior
there is a drama, a comedy,
and a tragedy.

— *The Refuge of the Derelicts*

Memory is a curious machine and strangely capricious. It has no order, it has no system, it has no notion of values, it is always throwing away gold and hoarding rubbish.

— *Three Thousand Years among the Microbes*

Nothing that grieves us can be called little: by the eternal laws of proportion a child's loss of a doll and a king's loss of a crown are events of the same size.

— *Which Was the Dream?*

Don't part with your illusions.
When they are gone you
may still exist but you have
ceased to live.

– Pudd'nhead Wilson

Human pride is not
worthwhile; there is always
something lying in wait to
take the wind out of it.

– *Following the Equator*

Humor is the great thing,
the saving thing after all.
The minute it crops up,
all our hardnesses yield,
all our irritations, and
resentments flit away, and a
sunny spirit takes their place.

— *What Paul Bourget Thinks of Us*

Against the assault of
laughter nothing can stand.

– *The Mysterious Stranger*

First published in 2018 by New Holland Publishers
London • Sydney • Auckland

131–151 Great Titchfield Street, London WIW 5BB, United Kingdom
1/66 Gibbes Street, Chatswood, NSW 2067, Australia
5/39 Woodside Ave, Northcote, Auckland 0627, New Zealand

newhollandpublishers.com

A record of this book is held at the British Library
and the National Library of Australia.

ISBN 9781742573809

Group Managing Director: Fiona Schultz
Publisher: Monique Butterworth
Proofreader: Kaitlyn Smith
Designer: Andrew Davies
Production Director: James Mills-Hicks
Printer: Toppan Leefung Printing Limited

1 3 5 7 9 10 8 6 4 2

Keep up with New Holland Publishers on Facebook
facebook.com/NewHollandPublishers